For those who have yet to come out.
There's a beautiful world awaiting you.
And, as always, for my trans friends.

"Who was I now—man or woman?
That question could never be answered
as long as those were the only two choices;
it could never be answered if it had to be asked."

- Leslie Feinberg, *Stone Butch Blues*

# GAY SEX

CHARLIE LOU EVANS

SIBLING RIVALRY PRESS
*DISTURB/ENRAPTURE*
LITTLE ROCK, ARKANSAS

Gay Sex

Cover art by Alder Schnabel
Cover design by Seth Pennington and Bryan Borland



Sibling Rivalry Press, LLC
159 Sunset Drive
North Little Rock, AR 72118
info@siblingrivalrypress.com
www.siblingrivalrypress.com

ISBN: 978-1-943977-98-7

First Sibling Rivalry Press Edition, June 2026

# GAY SEX



CONTENT NOTE:

*Some poems reference sexual violence, trauma, and dysphoria. These moments appear within a larger landscape of survival, tenderness, and queer becoming.*

## FUCKING AND UN-FUCKING MYSELF

I learned how to thrust my empty pelvis
against my mattress when I was eight years old,
before my body knew how to bleed,

before I became a woman.
When I was a genderless little faggot,
unconcerned with issues other than
flat bike tires and untied shoes,
without a name for anything
except the dragon figurines
guarding my nightstand.

Before I had a name for *it*.
When it was still a nameless pleasure found
in the core of me,
until I grew older, learned its name,
and my sex was used against me,
until I was pressed against steel countertops,
groped until I couldn't take it anymore.

And then I couldn't stop shoving
everything inside me.
Broom handles, pens, fingers, toothbrushes,
a cock with a curve on a god-fearing man,
the sweet lips of a soft poet,
a flaccid dick attached to a dear friend,

because if I shoved the whole world inside me,
it meant there was nothing on the outside
that could touch me anymore.

My life became a stream of bodies
attached to lovers,
attached to me in tangles of limbs
and sweat and forehead kisses and

hair brushed from lips and shuddering thighs.
I lost the ability to distinguish one from another
or myself from them.
Often times it was better that way,
sucked into the black hole of myself
our bodies bending on the event horizon
warping into a familiar warm
cyclical dance where time stopped
and all I could feel was *held*
by our soft bodies and raw humanity,
sticking to one another
through the long dark nights that yawned
before us like mouths.

Then one morning I stood alone
with my bare feet against the cool
hardwood floor of my bedroom,
loosened the leather straps of a harness,
tightened them and
slipped a glow-in-the-dark cock
through a steel ring
haloing my clit and began to rock back and forth,
thighs gripping a pillow,
hands gripping my new cock,
clit grinding,
breath panting,
my cock: a saber of light
my cock: streaming from the core of myself
my cock: the nameless formless pleasure
glowing softly between my fists,
my emptiness filled
as if my body had always known
before I did.
But of course it did.
My body had been thrusting me forwards
into a sweet eruption of a new life
since I was eight years old,

a genderless pleasure

where I am nothing

except filled

by myself.

## A RORSCHACH OF CUM

A Rorschach of cum spread across my chest.
Finally I could see the lawless shape of my future
pooling in the concave center of my ribcage,
thick, white clouds drifting towards my collarbones.
In this sticky mess: I knew I'd never be here again.
As he whistled around the room
and threw a towel at me
like I was an empty laundry machine,
I wiped off the ivory white glops pearling
around my iridescent breasts
and I imagined his chest on mine,
not in a sexy way,
but in the way I imagined my breasts to be,
as fluid as the clouds of his cum,
drifting off my chest
through the ceiling
and into the blue skies of tomorrow,
two small rainclouds
that would hold all the brilliant colors of the sunset
as I lay below them, lighter than air,
holding on to nothing at all,
free and fluid,
the weight of the world
off my chest,
disappearing through the ceilings
of men I never should've known
and wished I was.

## SEX TAPE

Every time a woman touches me, my brain flashes back through the last ten years of my sex life like a scratched VCR tape.

VCR tape rewinding: I watch a twenty-one year old crawl out from underneath a car where she went to cry after parties. The tears snake back up her face and rim her eyes like silver linings in the moonlight. She walks backwards into the frat house, ping pong balls floating back up into her palms like the reclaimed eyeballs of frat boys staring at her tits, eyes that would never see her as she saw herself, as one of them, as another boy. The vomit swirling up from the toilet, back into her red lips, pursing shut like a knife wound on her face, torn backwards into the bedroom, a man's naked body covering her like a morgue sheet, heavy bones holding her to the mattress, pulling himself out of her in a great unveiling, her body nude and untouched beneath him, soft as a streak of moonlight on the grey mattress covers, as if, like the moonlight, she slipped through his fingers. As if she birthed him as a man who never touched her, unmaking the mistake his mother made. Her quiet *no* tucked back inside of her mouth like a child into bedsheets. Like a body falling upwards from a suicide she rises from underneath him, her thin pale arms the bones of a bird taking flight. She stands next to him, taller somehow, even as he looks down at her.

The christian boy that tried
to fuck her queerness into hell
damning only himself.

The tape glitches, skips through dark nights where she spits cum back into soft cocks like white bullets, bodiless hands open their clutches, setting her free, over and over again. Un-fucking the men that fucked the man out of her. Each time she rises from below their faceless bodies, her body like a white dove flying from their obsidian bedrooms.

In the rewind, I see a new way of seeing love:
a closed fist opening.

In the rewind, blame is absolved from her. The blame I bruise into her skin is lifted along with bodiless hands, lifted along with faceless bodies. She never invited any of them in; she only saw them out, over and over, walking backwards out of doors that were never meant for her. In the rewind, instead of staring through the ceiling, she rises from the bedsheets. In the rewind, she takes her body back. In the rewind, she protects us.

It glitches again. She's sixteen, spitting out a cock in the parking lot, shoving the busboy backwards, his body thin and tired like a flickered-out streetlight in the dark. She walks backwards into the restaurant, puts her tips back in the jar, a couple unwrites their signature on the check, blue ink sucked back into the pen like a sharp breath, she walks white boxes full of their leftovers backwards into the kitchen, unboxing the bloody half-eaten meat as the waiters un-dig their fingers from her hips, un-grab her breasts, their arms snatching her back from a man with his wet mouth like the muzzle of a gun that brushes hers, all of them yanking their hands away like a firework of limbs, recoiling as if her skin burns them, their wanting expressions wiped from their faces like dirty tables. The dishwasher's phone slipped back into his pocket, his unforgivable erection softening as if he just remembered, she was only sixteen. She was only sixteen. She was *only sixteen*.

I was only sixteen.

All of this before my first kiss. Before my body was my own. Before I even knew what gender I was. It didn't matter whether or not I identified as a woman. I would still be fucked as one. It was always the same. His body pressed against my body using my body against me. All the men with their veined forearms and slim hips, reminding me with every grab, every bruise, every fuck that I could never be a man. They'd make sure of it. They clawed my insides until I ruptured into the woman they wanted. Shoved me into a gender I didn't pick just like their hands down my pants. Raped me until all I saw in the mirror was a sad girl, looking as hollow as the hole they fucked me into.

And that's what rape is about, isn't it?

It's not about the sex. It's about the christian boy trying to fuck the sin of my existence into hell. It's about my body being used as reassurance that transness isn't real. It's my queerness being molested as a consolation prize for these men that they're still needed. Needed? For what? For the flashback my body feels every time I'm touched? For the years of unlearning I have to do to love my own masculinity? For the men I continued to fuck because the most familiar love to me was abuse? No. There is no use for these men. They know it, too, which is why they try to hold me. Hit me. Rape me.

But they can do *nothing* to stop me from becoming who I am. *Fuck me all you want, I will still rise from the bedsheets to become a better man than you'll ever be.* I can understand women on a level you never will, because I understand what it feels like to be touched by you. And every time a woman touches me, all the pieces of me that were contorted by you begin to unravel.

The sex tape continues to rewind.

As the men's arms release the girl I used to be, her untouched body walks backwards through the revolving door, backwards until she was outside, the sun on her face, driving backwards down the winding road, Don Henley playing in reverse over the car speakers, "The Boys of Summer" gone, left behind where they can't reach her anymore, somewhere out over the rustling fields of corn flashing by her rolled-down windows, her laughter falling like sunlight on their open leaves, her fingers tracing the top of the horizon like wings, the days and nights reversing themselves, the cuts on her wrists closing like open mouths, her car ripping backwards from the restaurant, returning home to herself, her body her own, tucked into bedsheets, until he rises as a child again, his blue jean holes knitting themselves back together, dragons disappearing back into his crayons, frogs he raised turning back into tadpoles, walking backwards until he stands under a tree outside, a small bird with a broken wing cupped in his hands, until it falls back upwards into its nest, the bones in the wing unbreaking themselves, its small head looking skywards with its eyes latched on hope.

This, this is all the undoing I have undone in order to just be held by her. Because every time I am touched by a woman's hands, I remember all of the men who came before her. To let her softness in is to acknowledge all the roughness I've known.

Her gentle touch rewinds the tape every time
until I am undone into the man I've always been,

set free after all this time.

## COCK SNAKE

Tonight, I'm at the intersection of wanting a massive cock and worrying about growing a mustache.

Nightly after showering, I peel back the lips of my vagina like curtains to see if my clitoris has blossomed into anything longer. A kid isn't something I ever wanted to birth, but a cock...

One day, I peeled back my lips and a second head thrust forwards, sort of like a flesh snake erection, and it writhed around until the foreskin smoothed from its head, and it stared at me.

It was my face on the tip of my penis.
I was making eye contact with my own cock.
It blinked. I blinked.

And we went on like that
for about thirty minutes
until it told me it was hungry.

And so I just nodded and said, *well, alright. Let's go get some food.* And we ordered takeout and watched gynecologist porn on the TV and wondered why we got off so much on the women getting off on the men who were fucking them like it was part of a routine exam. Maybe it was the fact that the women "didn't know" what was going on. Maybe it was the fact that when I turned away from pleasure, I could feel it better. When I wasn't making eye contact with my own cock, I could touch it. When I ignored the mountains of my breasts, I could see your eyes. If I looked at my own body, the pleasure burst, dissipated, and I was strangled by the flesh snake of my own making.

Sometimes it swallowed me whole and my cock replaced my own head. Sometimes during sex, I wouldn't even be there. It would just be this cock snake, and my exes never could tell the difference, so it didn't matter.

The cock snake churned into any number of positions. It morphed into a girl bent over, into the women getting fucked by the men like a routine exam, into a hole a man could fuck and I was somewhere at the end of that hole, getting rammed into the shapes they pleased. And then, at the end, the cock snake would recede back into me, and I would coil into a small spiral of despair on wet sheets.

It wasn't like that with you. With you, the cock snake emerged, but I was kissing you and wrestling it at the same time. When I cried, it was because I could feel it starting to eat me. I cried because I hated being taken away from you. This was the first time I acknowledged its presence during sex instead of just letting it have its way. I wouldn't have acknowledged it if you hadn't seen it, too. You were the first one that ever had.

Once it felt known, it stopped trying to eat me, and curled around you with me instead, wrapping us tighter together, until our shapes fit each other perfectly. It let me slip free of my body, just like it would a month later, when it emerged from my clitoris after a shower. Some might think I should've strangled it when it emerged on its own, but really, I was just glad we were finally getting along.

It came out because it got confused. It thought there was a man around, but it was just me. Now we change together into the shapes we please. We're shedding our skin and changing into something that can change with you.

# THAT TIME EVERYTHING TURNED INTO COCKS

No shoes, no license,
we're buying wine and we're late.
We're parallel parking for thirty minutes and
pissing everyone off in a ten-car pileup behind us,
but fuck them.
Let's kiss the next time I pull backwards.
All the angry horns will form a symphony of
music to the ears of lovers
who just don't give a fuck.

You've thrown your phone out the window
and I've run over it, and we're ditching the car
mid-rush hour and breaking
all the traffic rules and running
up the stairs to your apartment,
fucking to the tune of car alarms.

You're sucking my clit and it's turning into a cock.
I'm fingering you and my fingers turn into cocks.
Our clits are rubbing against each other
and turning into cocks,
and everything is turning into cocks,
especially our whole entire bodies,
throbbing, engorged members twining around
each other like freak pink slugs,
veins bulging like rivers of blood passion.

And when we cum, the whole room is slicked,
and we slither out the door and into the streets,
giant cum slug cocks slicking down the sidewalks
past the cars, zipping into grocery stores shoeless,
where we steal the cheapest bottles of wine and
crack them open with our snake cock bodies
because fuck knows where a bottle opener is,

because fuck knows how long
I've waited to feel this alive.

Drunk on the joys of having junk
that can be anything,
on the sweet rapture of having
a partner that knows
how to suck you into a new gender
and fuck you into oblivion
till there's nothing left to think about,
nothing but the small weight
of their head on your chest
and how none of it really matters
once you've found someone to
slick it with.

# THE INFINITE FIELD OF SPRING

I sit across from her at the table.
Our eyes lock, half open like moons.
We have not slept in days.

Every night we walk through a field of white tulips,
emptying petal cups full of the things we are
learning about one another.

In the car, we pass sweetness between our lips,
tucked into squares of dark chocolate pressed from
her mouth into mine. It makes my face twist until
it becomes hers, and we are staring back at each
other in the rearview mirror, mistaking her hands
for mine on the steering wheel. I do not know
who is driving or when we started or where we are
going or who is in control or if we will crash,

but I am thinking about my hand balanced
on the inner seam of her blue jeans
like a tightrope walker.

I am thinking about how she whispered on a
crosswalk, *I understand why people make such
a big deal out of being gay*, and she could only
realize that now, holding my hand.

(How great it felt to be a part of that hand!)

Walking through downtown streets, full of cars and
eyes and hands that could never fit
the way ours do,
the way our softness intertwines, softer than petals,
softer than whispers,

but obvious as a stoplight that

we did not have to live the way everyone
else did, we did not have to have
husbandkidsjobhousefamily.

We could just have each other,

for today, walking on a sunny afternoon,
breathing in bits of each other's lives,
hand in hand through an infinite field of spring.

## CHERRY BLOSSOMS

I covered your thighs
in the soft pink petals of a cherry tree,
clustered them at your abdomen,
laced them between the thin blue rivers
of the veins on your forearms,
and I placed one on your head
like a small pink hat that kept falling.

You were explaining to me your parents,
who threw heavy things across rooms,
heaved their ugly voices over your own
until you were screaming in a room
that never felt like home.

I was trying to cover you with the lightest things
I could find so that maybe together
we could drift up into the springtime air,
held aloft by the soft pink petals that looked like
the insides of our cheeks, that looked like
a thousand tiny sails, that looked like
your hand cupped in mine in a bath of sunlight.

But you panicked
and shook the flowers from your body,
petals falling like pink tears.

I realized no matter how light they were
you would always feel their weight.

## FOUR POEMS FOR A THREESOME

Our fingers trace the outlines of our bodies,
shading the slim shadow in your abdomen
or cupping the pool of light in your collarbone.
Before we had touched,
all I had known were lovers
who erased me with rough hands
and blotted out my hips with bruises until my
whole body dissolved into shadow.

Now I lie between you both
with my eyes closed,
feeling you trace me back into existence
one fingertip at a time, our tattoos crawling over
one another,
losing track of whose limbs are whose,
redrawing ourselves as one.

***

I find myself wishing I had three mouths
or that we all had one mouth or that
my body was covered in mouths for us all to kiss,
dozens of lips brushing softly against one another
tenderly as butterfly wings opening and closing,
like a pine tree covered in monarchs,
like a new future metamorphosing
and migrating from the colder
parts of me.

***

Our hands meet like two strangers
on the abdomen of our lover,
circling around his core
in a slow dance.

How tender that the room
our hands dance in
for the first time
is the softest part
and the center of our love.

***

If lesbian sex is an infinite field,
then sex between three trannies
is the river I float home on,
bedsheets moving in silken waves
as my mouth fills with his clit.
We melt into raindrops falling
into the same current:

downstream, there is hope.
I know it.

## THE INFINITE CIRCUIT OF FAGGOTRY

My head cranes backward against the earth.
As I look up I see you,
white body soft as clouds,
swan neck arching above me,
breasts like twin teardrops of the midnight sun.

Your hair swept back into a ponytail,
tongue and teeth cupping all that is soft
and good between my palms.
We are knuckles deep past things
we can grasp,
the curve of your hips accenting mine
like parentheses.

(Between us we keep safe
what has been torn from us by men.
Between us we are growing something
softer than children,
softer than breasts or hips or skin.)

It is everything unsaid. Everything wordless.
We are cocooned in it,
the tender loop of our bodies,
infinite in the soft pleasure
of filling the empty places in one another
we thought no one could ever reach.

Beside me, inside me,
you are curled into a pale question mark,
asking the unanswerable,
just how, murmuring through your lips into mine,
how have we managed to find one another.

My fingers slide inside you like an outlet and
I am electrified.

We form an infinite circuit of faggotry,
lit up like the new sun,
the faggot sun of the new age,
a rising portal anyone can step through
and become faggot sons
in the golden light of our dawn.

With us there is no such thing as gender.

There is only the constant filling and unfilling
of you into me and me into you,
like vases with flowers or the sky with clouds or
doorways with all the familiar lovers you thought
you had lost forever, only to find filling you softly
once again in a half-stranger's hand.

How beautiful it is:

the filling and emptying of ourselves like buckets.

I feel the pleasure in reaching,
outstretched fingers like tree branches
growing toward the light and the clouds
that kiss leaves softly in the sweet summer rain.

# A PAIR OF LOVESICK HERMAPHRODITES

My body finds yours. I blink and suddenly
my world is upside down. We are spiraling.
We have become two slugs, enmeshed,
cascading, wrapping tightly around one another
like two hands holding.

In slug time, we can slow things down
to dance a little longer. Feel a little deeper.
This risky upside-down business,
this slow eroticism of your touch,
this sweet unfurling of one another,
may we intertwine until
there is no up or down anymore,
until everything settles into a delicious molasses,
until our slick bodies shift through the genders
just to fit inside one another.

How lovely to find another person to change with.

Your shoulder mistaken for my hip, my mouth
mistaken for your lips,

a pair of lovesick hermaphrodites, are we not?

An endless genderfuck, a puddle of limbs
all trying to dissolve into one another.

As a slug, I gave up my bones
a long time ago in hopes
of finding someone to hold like this.

As a slug I can tell you,
and I know you will understand,
that I am in no hurry,
because I know we have all the time in the world.

# LET'S KEEP DOING THINGS WHERE THEY'RE NOT SUPPOSED TO BE DONE:

Screaming erotic poems in the bowling alley,
opening each other's love letters in libraries,
fucking in the kitchen
till our bellies are full of the kind of
pleasure that coats our insides with
pulsating ecstasy.

Feeling warmth curl into our stomachs like
purring cats.

Smoke alarms whine, but
I am deaf between the walls of your naked thighs
pressed against the
wood countertops like cookie dough.

Dinner is well past done.
Everything is burning,
charred in the oven.

To me there is only the rosemary in your hair
and the rhythmic waves of your breath
pulling me under and over and through you
and into you, and everything becomes you,
and the only dinner I want to eat
on a deserted island is you,
and you a thousand times over.

You where you are not supposed to be,
splayed on my kitchen counter
between the radishes and ginger.

You where I least expect it,
knees knocking like bowling pins
as we roll into one another.

You coming and going through my life,
whispering as light as the rustling of book pages
that you know this story,
that you have been here before,
that you know me and have known me
for as long as I have been alive,
and know that all I have ever wanted
is to be known.

Known, but especially by you.

And your burnt casserole,
after which we will go to bed
sharing a hunger
that is more satiating than any meal
I have ever known.

## TWO DYKES SHARING UNDERWEAR

Our love feels like we are reaching toward each
other with our eyes closed.

Like a strange homoerotic game
of hide and go seek,
it is my underwear under your clothes, the same
fabric that holds the hot, wet parts of me
holding the hot, wet parts of you,
our innermost caverns cupped together
like two open mouths, lip to lip,

kissing or screaming or sighing or laughing
all at once, experiencing this life jaw wide open,
letting the flies in and the birds and the bees and a
whole strip club of gay men and even the bouncer
and the odd fellow in the corner carving spoons
and a couple of cat women in latex suits.

Our love is about letting it all in.
It is about the fact that you cannot see it,
but it is closest to you,
closest even to the most sensitive parts of you.

You are the second person to wear a pair of my
underwear. The first was my christian ex-boyfriend.
Except the underwear he wore was my red lace
thong and, looking back at it, it was more fitting
for him than it was for me,
not that he would ever understand that.

With you, it is different.
You are wearing a pair of my boxers,
and it fits both of us because, on some level,
it is who we are.

And you can see me for that,
which is more than he ever could.
Which is more than I ever thought possible.
Which is more than I ever thought I deserved.

There is so much I used to beg for.
There is so much I used to beg for
that it makes it difficult
to look directly at this blatant wanting,
this need for you,

because I am so afraid that if I turn to look
it will all be too good to be true
and you will be gone.

However, every time I have peeked,
you are still there.
Still real. As persistent as my disbelief.

This is the best hide and go seek
I have ever played, because at any given time
one of us is hiding and one of us is searching
and both of us are being perpetually found
by each other.

There is an internalized homophobia and
transphobia that I am breaking through all at once
because of how badly I want to hold you. Those
are the names of the things that make me hide
under the table, thinking everyone had given up
searching a while ago. They are the things that
make me close my eyes during sex as if I were
about to be clocked with a right hook,
except the blow
never comes,

only I do and you do,
and there is so, so much pleasure
where there used to be pain.

I realize everything is different with you
because with you I am changing into
who I want to become.
These things we tease out of each other are the
heartstrings that braid our lives together.

Everything is different with you,
because when I imagine sex with you
I imagine us in your room, myself draped over your
legs like a white curtain in the breeze,
quivering with each touch of your windy fingers,
the sun shining through me,
everything warm.

I want you to take me there.

## HOW FAR WE'VE COME

My cold hands warmed on your hips,
swaying with you to an acoustic guitar
in the top left window of the house on the bay,
with the tree with heart-shaped leaves
that filter all the light crimson
and speckled into your
morning sunroom,

where the two lovers
sway with their heads buried
in each other's shoulders,
thinking how beautiful,

thinking of past lovers in dark rooms,
in basements with sweat-drenched walls,
bass flooded and cum-stained,
the hands that clenched until hips bruised,
the bodies that thrust until
consent became a lost whisper for mercy,
until all the light left
and my body was a memory
I remember now,
in your arms,
held,
thinking:

how beautiful,

how beautiful
how far we have come.

## REDWOOD TEARS

On the coast of Arcata, California,
a flock of sandpipers
skirts the flat lace of a wave
pressing itself into the shore.

Ocean mist kisses the wet boughs of the redwoods
in the golden morning light until they cry,
and tiny gold tears fall
from them
to the top of my hair
and down my cheeks
as I watch the ocean fold into itself over and over
while it traces cold rivers through my hair,
gathers on my eyelashes,
and falls into the redwood roots
I stand on,
that we stood on,

when we stood inside
the blackened jaw of one severed stump,
its smooth soot walls reflecting soft
darkness against the hollows of your cheeks.

The wildfire that once ravaged its insides
has long since turned damp and slick with lichen,
your neck craned backward,
mouth open,
a small crater of pleasure
to the sky
full of branches
holding one another,

as my fingers pushed
inside you,
reaching,

as your tide pressed itself
into me,
folding
us into each other
over and over

until we lapsed back into
ocean tears that seeped
quietly into the redwood roots
that will forever hold us
long after one of us is gone.

## THE LAST STAINS OF YOU

I fucked you until your hair
became a knot of the words we could not say,
the physical manifestation of our grief,
tangled where neither of us could see
but both of us could feel,
written in our tangled split ends.

*This felt like saying goodbye,*
you said as I withdrew my fingers
from inside you, and they stuck together
with your blood in two crimson rings
around my two innermost fingers.

I threw the sheets in the wash as you stumbled
into the kitchen, sat down,
and blankly stared at me
with bloodshot eyes, hair sticking out like
broken elbows from your head.

I could not let you leave that way.

At the blue checkered kitchen table,
I stood behind you, tugging a hairbrush gingerly
through the mess I made trying to fuck any doubt
from your mind that we could not be one forever.

I thought of all the days my mom stood behind me
brushing my hair, untangling knots, tying it back
in a white ribbon, bunny-earing my shoelaces,
driving me to school,
watching me grow up,
letting me go.

And here I stand behind you,
untangling the knotted parts of myself

from knotted parts of yourself you cannot see,
smoothing your soft brown hair,
thinking of the child in me
loving the child in you,
hugging you tightly in my doorframe
and letting you go.

That night,
after you are gone,
I make my bed with clean sheets
only to find a permanent bloodstain
in the center of the bed
where our bodies
failed to become one,
but now have
in the way I never wanted,
with you tangled in my mind
as I lie alone,
restless,
kept warm
by the last stains
of you.

## THE SPACE BETWEEN SOMEDAY AND TODAY

In our separate beds, 600 miles away,
I know we are still intertwined in
each other's minds.

It does not make any sense
to continue a relationship
when we will never share a home,
only this incessant longing.

You cannot root a garden in wishful thinking
or lose a security deposit on lust,
and you definitely cannot
slam the door on yearning.

Our love, sustained on desperation,
will consume itself
and us.

This is why,
even as I have left you,
nothing has changed.

I feel just as close to you
from 600 miles away
as when we were together,
because you were never here at all,
just the voice on the other end of the line
I reached for and felt nothing for so long
that it began to feel like everything
until I woke up to realize

as long as my mind is tangled with yours
my bed will remain empty.

Of course,
there is still a deranged part of me that chants
*someday, maybe someday,*
like I can summon you from
beneath my skin
(god knows how many times
we have tried to crawl inside each other
and failed),
but the truth is

I cannot build a future off of somedays,
and it is too early to make it today,
so what can one do
except leave you
in yesterdays
with the hope
that there will be a someday
when I wake up
next to you
every day.

Until then I will rise
to intertwine myself
in today.

## IN QUEERNESS NO ONE IS EVER LOST

In this strange queerness,
no one is ever lost.
When I hold a lover's hand, I hold all
the lovers I've held before. All
our old memories remain tucked
beneath my skin like old letters
she unfolds tenderly and reads back to me
until I fall asleep, smiling
at how beautiful the insides of me feel
on her lips. Each time I enter a body,
I kneel before a temple of everyone
I have ever loved, tonguing my adoration
into the cavern between their thighs,
a strange well my love note wishes
are whispered into:

*that you all will always be held the way I am,*
*that the way I hold you*
*was the way I held her*
*was the way I held them,*
*is the way I will hold everyone, forever,*
*whenever they fall into my arms.*

## A FOOT IN THE DOOR

You walked into my life
as if I had left a door open the whole time.

One day there you were:
the warmth in my bedsheets,
laughter in my kitchen,
a foot in the doorway.
Like an imaginary friend that became real,
taking all of the best pieces of me
and materializing to hold my hand
on summer afternoons.

Appearing with a new comforter after I told you
how much I hated my blue one. Now there
is an orange comforter in my room, recovered
from the depths of your closet, and it fills my walls
with a rusty orange like an eternal sunset.
Without even being under it,
it keeps me warm.

We pickpocket nothing from each other's pants.
My fingers have already found all the love notes
you have tucked into my bed. Still they search past
the dryer lint and crumpled receipts to the warmth
of your thighs, the curve of your body cupped in
my fingers, retrieving nothing
but holding everything.

We hide our smiles in each other's shoulders
as we sway in the clumsy brightness of the
afternoon, drunk on the shaft of sunlight
illuminating both of our heads like candle flames.

We flicker in and out of one another in front of
the stove as the pasta cooks, overcooks, boils over.

*There was so much I used to beg for that you just do,* I whispered into the softness of your neck.

*Honey, we're gay now,* you said back.

Your eyes are bright like windows thrown open
to the sky. Your face softened in the afternoon
light. I never realized the chairs in my house
were so empty without you.

Above the table where we share dinner, we fool
the world into thinking we are two people. Below
the table our legs braid into a pair of knotted
shoelaces. We are going nowhere, all tied up,
my thighs tangled in your knees, your shins
pressed against my anklebones.

Useless to our main functions,
but finding better entanglements.
Our hands practice sensual thumb wrestling
above the table. Neither of us wins.

Our fingertips' grooves kiss
until they form new ones,
a hundred tiny caverns
all fitting together
as if you folded the Grand Canyon in half
and everything mysteriously lined up in a
beautiful mess of rust-colored orange.

It is a sunset I could watch forever.
It is a sunset I will watch forever,
gazing at the walls of my room,
remembering when the chair
at my kitchen table
used to be full.

## ABOUT THE POET

Charlie Lou Evans (he/they) grew up in New Jersey, graduated from Virginia Tech, and currently lives in Bellingham, Washington. They explore gender and sexuality through poetry, and find it most fulfilling when others see themselves in their work.

This is their debut chapbook.

**www.charlielouevans.net**

## ABOUT THE PRESS

Sibling Rivalry Press is an independent press based in Little Rock, Arkansas, with a mission to publish work that disturbs and enraptures. It is a sponsored project of Fractured Atlas, a nonprofit arts service organization. Contributions to support the operations of Sibling Rivalry Press are tax-deductible to the extent permitted by law, and your donations will directly assist in the publication of work that disturbs and enraptures. To contribute to the publication of more books like this one, please visit our website and click *donate*.

**www.siblingrivalrypress.com**

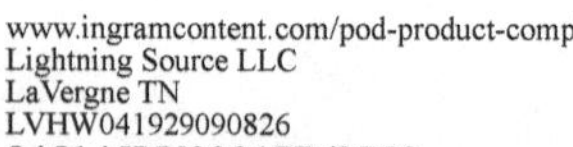
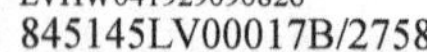
www.ingramcontent.com/pod-product-compliance
Lightning Source LLC
LaVergne TN
LVHW041929090826
845145LV00017B/2758

* 9 7 8 1 9 4 3 9 7 7 9 8 7 *